BLACK SHADOWS

AND THROUGH THE

WHITE LOOKING GLASS

BLACK SHADOWS

AND THROUGH THE

WHITE LOOKING GLASS

Remembrance of Things Past and Present

WILLIAM E. WATERS

authorHOUSE®

AuthorHouse™
1663 Liberty Drive
Bloomington, IN 47403
www.authorhouse.com
Phone: 1-800-839-8640

Published by AuthorHouse   03/06/2013

ISBN: 978-1-4817-2288-9 (sc)
ISBN: 978-1-4817-2287-2 (e)

Library of Congress Control Number: 2013903781

This book is printed on acid-free paper.

In memoriam:
Constance E. Waters
(1933-1978)

Proverbs 31:2

At Books and Books today I ran my hand over the spines lined up on a shelf, the multicolored text—backbones of people's fears and imaginations. My fingernails painted gaudy like butterflies embarrassed me. I felt like a *puta* at a church, not really fitting in but wanting the hushed reverence, the knowledge of mysteries. I close my eyes and pulled one out at random: *Remembrance of Things Past*—and I wanted to know, to ask somebody wise like the priest of the bookstore, whether it is true that the past really passes, because today, I have the feeling that it doesn't. That we just pretend.

Lisette Mendez
"Remembrance of Things Present"

In truth, our history was *not* knowing; it was being shielded from the truth. That was the American way.

—James Patterson

Preamble

From slavery to freedom.
From pre-colonialism to post-modernism.
From revolution to reactionism.
From the War for Independence
        to the Civil War
From the slave enlistment bill
        to Selective Service.
From Articles of Confederation
        to the Confederacy.
From agrarianism to technocratism.
From pre-industrialization.
        to post-industrialization

From George Washington
        to George Bush.
From the birth of a nation
        to a kinder, gentler nation.
From Thomas Jefferson
        to William Jefferson Clinton.
From Democratic Republicanism
        to the New Democrats.
From honest Abe
        to tricky Dick
        to Slick Willie.
From preserving the Union
        to fighting a "lawless society"
        to establishing a New Covenant.
From Radical Republicanism
        to Roosevelt's reign
        to Reaganism.

From Reconstruction
>   to public works
>   to trickle-down economics.

From the Welfare State
>   to a Police State.

From the Do Nothing Party
>   to the Freedom Now Party.

From New Deal Democrats
>   to Dixiecrats.

From the Grand Old Party
>   to the Great Society
>   to this dialogue on race.

From the melting pot
>   to multiculturalism.

From Jim Crow
>   to the Rainbow Coalition.

From Griots to the Last Poets

From Phillis Wheatley
>   to Gwendolyn Brooks.

From highly imitative
>   to Pulitzer Prize-winning poetry.

From *Various* Subjects, *Religious and Moral*
>   to *Annie Allen*.

From Zora Neale Hurston
>   to Toni Morri*son*.

From Th*eir Eyes Were Watching God*
>   to Para*dise*.

From folklore
>   to Nobel Laureate fiction.

From *Mules and Men*
>   to *Beloved*.

From Richard Wright
　　to James Baldwin
　　to Walter Mosley.
From *Native Son*
　　to "Sonny's Blues"
　　to *A Devil in a Blue Dress*.

From the Royal Family—
Count Basie, Duke Ellington
and Nat King Cole
　　to the King of Pop.
From a Lady singing the blues
　　to the Funky Divas.
From the Queen of Soul
　　to Queen Latifah.
From Bojangles
　　to M.C. Hammer
　　to the Tap Dance Kid.
From *Porgy and Bess*
　　to *Jelly's Last Jam*.
From slave songs and spirituals
　　to soul.
From delta blues
　　to rhythm and blues.
From New Orleans jazz
　　to Brass Construction.
From ragtime
　　to rock 'n' roll
　　to rap.

The gift of story and song.

From slavery
　　　to sharecropping.
From pickin' cotton
　　　to hoeing fields.
From the farm
　　　to the factory.
From grapes of wrath
　　　to industrial traps.
From the plantation
　　　to the penitentiary.
From the old slavery
　　　to the new slavery.
From chattel slavery
　　　to the convict lease system
　　　to the chain gang
　　　to prisons for profit.

The gift of sweat and brawn.

From Africa to America.
From chains to the cross.
From a slave religion
　　　to a religion of salvation.
From segregated balconies
　　　to the front of the pews.
From hearing the Word
　　　to proclaiming it.
From making a way out of no way
　　　to leading the way.

The gift of the spirit.

The long shadows
of black history in America,
once hidden, often denied,
now revealed.

I

In the beginning
there was slavery.
Before the white man
came to Africa
there was slavery.
Even today in Africa
there's slavery.
Slavery's an ancient African tradition.

Slavery's associated with
descendants of Africans,
though the word "slave"
comes from "Slav,"
a Germanic people who were enslaved.

Millions of people
were snatched
from the bosom
of Mother African
to be enslaved.

An eternity has passed
since chained Africans
stepped off of slave ships
with Christian names
to toil on the lang.
Mostly their blood,
but their sweat and their tears,
fertilized this new world.

Although more Africans
first went to the "West Indies"—
to be "broken in"—
Brazil and the Spanish Empire,
when we think of slavery,
we think of America,
"land of the free . . . ."

Slavery's long been called
America's "original sin."
American Adams and Eves
ate from the tree
of the knowledge of good and evil
and chose evil.

American slavers harvested
and ate in slavery's garden,
the white man's Paradise,
the black man's Hell.

They couldn't get enough.
There was an insatiable passion
driving the slave trade,
for more and more
of this strange fruit.
There was a hunger
for black bodies
that haunts us to this day.

We live in the shadows
of this history.

II

On the auction blocks,
male and female and even child,
bronze bodies oiled and buffed,
prepared to be sold
like used furniture.
Bare black breasts weighed
with rough white hands,
squeezed like fruit.
Teeth exposed,
dirty white fingers
rubbed across pink gums.
Large, piano-shaped
ivory teeth tapped,
new music emanating
from this mouth forced open—
the gift of song.
The span of hips
measured with lecherous eyes,
calculating the number
of children she can bear.

Demure white ladies
who'd insisted to come along,
hatted and veiled,
fan in hands,
covering their faces
up 'til their eyes,
batting them in disbelief
at the strange fruit hanging
from sturdy tree trunk-like
ebony legs.

Their eyes did their
own calculating,
sized them up.
Was it possible to—
no, impossible!
A lady couldn't
she just couldn't.
They had to stifle screams
just at the thought of it.

There were screams.
Screams as they were taken
        from Mother Africa.
Screams as they were shackled
        in holding pens.
Screams as they were forced
        on slave ships.
Screams as they jumped
        to their death,
        into the waiting arms
        of the deep,
        or into the jaws of sharks
        who knew the itinerary
        of the triangular trade.
Screams in the holds of ships,
        where the rapes began.
Screams when they alighted
        on foreign land.
Screams when they were separated
        and placed on auction blocks.
Screams at the bodily invasions.
Screams in the slave quarters,
        where the rapes continued.

Screams when they're beaten
        into submission,
'til they're beaten into silence.

These screams are now
thought to be silent,
but they can still be heard.
They echo off the walls of history.
They are remembered and relived
in the collective unconscious.
They can still be seen,
in every woman of color,
the different shades of color—
fifty-five strains.
Look deeply into her eyes.
See the past reflected there.
Glance at the descendants
of the children
she was forced to bear.
And scream,
                scream,
            scream.

III

In the beginning
there was flesh,
firm sun-burnt flesh.
It ignited the passions
of cold-blooded white men
who'd have their way.

They feasted their eyes
on black Venuses
with bodies molded for love—
hourglass figures,
Hottentot rumps.

White men wouldn't be denied;
they forced themselves upon them.

The brutal lust of white men,
unleashed on unwilling black women,
again and again and again.
No respite from their lust.
No sanctuary for their bodies.
Slave cabins' doors
always opened.
Spectral-like,
the whites of their
eyes gleaming;
predators' teeth
revealed through
the crack of leers.

They invaded cabins,
invaded their bodies.
Holy temples violated,
defiled again and again and again.
This bloody altar of lust,
at which black womanhood
was violated and sacrificed,
again and again and again.
Pregnant from these rapes,
children called pickaninnies.

Slavery,
perpetrated and perpetuated
at this altar.
Black maidens
turned into cabin prostitutes,
a bizarre "Christian" ritual
reminiscent of paganism,
of temple prostitution
and fertility cults.

A nation of bastards
conceived by rape.
To the fields these children went,
along with their mothers,
like beasts of burden—
mulattos ("mules")—
while their "fathers" oversaw them
toiling in the sun.

Forced to bear children
white "fathers" wouldn't claim,
again and again and again,
children bred

to labor in the fields,
like mules,
some mothers took
their newborns' lives—
an act of mercy,
freed from bondage in this way.

Did would-be slave children
mercy-killed by their mothers
eat pie in the sky,
or were their souls lost forever,
their bodies reborn
to slavery everlasting?

It didn't matter.
Those children not sacrificed
by weak or loving mothers
carried the burden,
"the curse of Ham,"
one of many
religious justifications
for slavery.

IV

Babies snatched from mothers' milk,
too young to stand on their own.
Sometimes they were sold,
to a master down the road—
it really didn't matter,
the bond had been broken
'tween mother and child.

The child was born and bred
to labor in the fields,
never to know
the carefreeness of youth.
Strapped to his or her mother's back,
wrapped in rags,
swaddled from the sun.
No lullabies, but "slave songs,"
or "spirituals," if you will,
sung by black angels in the field,
their children heard
from can't see in the morning
'til can't see at night—
these mothers sang
and carried their double burden,
as they toiled in the fields.

No burden too great
did these mothers escape;
they labored in fields with men.
They were the objects
of wanton white-hot lust,
but denied the privilege of womanhood.
That was reserved for white women,
as they swooned
under the scorching heat
in their hats and veils
and in layers of petticoats
to protect them
from their own men's lust.

They drank iced tea
brought to them
on silver platters
by mulatto children
who resembled their husbands.

They were privileged
but not preferred;
black wenches had
that dubious distinction.
Their pretty bronze faces
and shapely bodies
were constantly swollen
from unwanted
invasions of their wombs
by this alien race of men.

Black women bore
the lust of white men,
and the anger of white women.
Mistreated, beaten
even with child in womb;
forced to lie across a "belly ditch"
to protect slavery's posterity,
they were lashed across their backs.
They got the message,
and the unborn children, too.
This is a message
that informs us to this day.
Living in the long shadow
of this history.

V

Their husbands' bastards ("mules")
laboring in the fields
with their mothers
must've diminished
their respect for their men.
Some were first-borns,
denied the inheritance,
treated like animals.

Only the privilege
of their fair skin,
their feigned indifference
and "weakness,"
and available and defenseless
black women
in abundance,
saved white women
from the same fate.
They were left alone,
to dream fairy tales,
to live privileged lives,
their femininity idolized
but their sexuality diminished,
while their men flaunted
their sexcapades
with nigger wimmin.

In constrictive clothing,
petticoats and corsets,
their sexuality confined,
while barely dressed black women
unconsciously flaunted firm flesh;
pointy breasts, chiseled waists
without the benefit
of corsets,
sculpted buttocks
and legs tapered
for flight—
they put Venus to shame.

Later suffragettes
would make this connection,
that their sexual subjugation,
their duty to give
their husbands' sons
to continue the
family name,
was akin to slavery.
Not quite,
nowhere near the reality,
but the evidence of their men's
arrogance and contempt for women,
even nigger wimmin,
was always before their eyes—
a nation of bastards,
chained and rarely clamed
by their men
who boasted Southern gentility.

VI

Something happened,
something very strange happened.
The base desire white men had
for black bodies was transmuted.
In their preference for black flesh
they saw their justification.

A Turkish saying:
A white woman to please the eye;
and an Egyptian and a black one
for sexual pleasure.

Sicilian:
Femmina scura; femmina amursa.
(A dark woman is a passionate woman.)

Portuguese:
*Branca para casar
mulata para f . . .
Negra para trabljar.*
(White woman for marriage,
mulatto woman for sexual pleasure,
black woman for work.)

(Black women called:
property;
brood-sow;
work-ox;
mule.)

But it all began
with black women,
this bastardization.
Was the white man
trying to extinguish his lust
for the black woman by breeding
the black woman into one
indistinguishable from a white one?

The white man bred black women
and produced the mulatto;
he bred mulattos
and produced the quadroon;
he bred quadroons
and produced the octoroon;
he bred octoroons
and produced a white woman
with "black blood" flowing
through her veins.

From the African, Caucasian and Indian—
from this unrestrained rape—
fifty-five different strains were conceived.

Pardos.

Mestizo;
quinteron de mestizo;
requinteron de mestizo;
blanco.

Mulatto;
quadroon or quadroon of mulatto;
quinteron de mulatto or octoroon;
requinteron de mulatto.

Mulatto;
zambo, sambo or lobo;
cuateron or quadroon.

Coyote.

Cambuja;
sambahiga;
calpamulatto or chino;
givero.

Creoles;
caboclos;
chinos;
jibaros.

Gens de couleur;
sang mele—
"mixed bloods."

Chinos del pais.
Cafuso;
mameluco (mameloque);
musterfino;
metis.

Congos;
creole Negroes.

Etc., etc., etc.

Today, people say,
what should we call ourselves?
African-Americans?
Descendants of
Africans, Caucasians and Indians.

Fifty-five different strains.

Pardos.

A bastard nation,
conceived by rape.

VII

White men's greatest fear,
was that black men
would do to white women
what white men
had done to black women—
rape them.

A suggestion of
sexual impropriety,
even a wayward glance—
"reckless eyeballing"—
would bring on
an horrific punishment.
Boiled alive, flayed,
and oh!, yes, castrated.

Was it penis envy,
the almost
mythical huge proportions
of the black male's organ
that inspired this fury?
If bigger was better,
then where did that
leave the white man?

And was the white woman
so pure, so chaste—
was she unaffected
by the unrestrained rape
of black women
by her man?
Out of resentment,
did she want
to taste
the forbidden fruit?
Did she flirt
with this strange idea,
did she present opportunities
for the African slave
to feast on her white body
with his eyes?
In this sexually charged
atmosphere,
did she understand
her craving,
her calculating,
or her desire for revenge
on her mate?
Was it revenge,
or pure lust?
Nature knows no color lines.

Was her passionate nature denied,
suppressed until
she acted out?
Was she really cold,
an ice goddess?
Was she merely to look at,
perched on a pedestal,
to idealize in marriage,
too pure for a lusty romp
in the sack?

His sheer physicality
could be overwhelming.
It inspired a certain admiration,
even in his wretchedness.
There was always that special one,
a swagger still in his walk,
if one watched closely,
a potential leader of a rebellion.
His docility and acceptance
of his lot feigned.
It was in the eyes,
if one bothered to look.
They were dark and smoldering
with black rage.
He would take her,
not out of lust or desire
but revenge.
He would do to her
what white men
did to black women.

He would have no mercy,
would kill her
if he could
get away with it.
There was a certain fatal
attraction there.
To even flirt with her
was to tempt death.
She could have him whipped
for the look in his eyes;
she could have him castrated
for the way he looked at her.
She could have him boiled alive.
She could have him killed
if it struck her fancy.

Laws were passed.
White women caught
in flagrante delicto
with black males
would be enslaved themselves,
along with their children.
It was already a tradition
that children of any union
between blacks and whites
were "black"—
they had "black blood."
They were thus slaves.
Black skin became
synonymous with slavery.

William E. Waters

Even after slavery
white men passed laws to deny
black men access
to white women's bodies—
"white slavery."
Black on white was seen
as sexual subjugation.
White women had to be protected
from their passion,
black men punished for it.

It mattered not if he was
a slave or the reigning
heavyweight champ,
or some chump on the streets;
it mattered not if she was
a slave mistress,
or the daughter of financiers,
or poor white trash—
there was a price they both
had to pay.

The long shadow of history
haunts us to this day.
It can be seen
when a black male
and a white female
are seen together in public.
There's the evil eye
from black women,
utter contempt
from white men.

It can be seen
when a black female
and a white male
are seen together in public.
There's evil words
from black men,
astonished looks
from black women.
They all stand guilty,
hiding in the shadows of history,
white men as rapists,
white women as silent co-conspirators,
black men as cowards,
black women as compliant victims.
This brought them together
as much as it pulled them apart.
Slavery was as much abut sex
as it was about subjugation.

VIII

In West Africa today,
slaves, mostly female,
are still subjugated.
It's an ancient
African tradition.
Girls, as young as seven,
are enslaved in Ghana,
given by family members
to men of the gods
to atone for crimes
committed by relatives.

A *trokosi*—
wife or slave of the gods—
is given to a tribal priest,
her virginity sacrificed
to appease the gods,
so we are told,
while pedophiliac priests
grin lecherously,
their lust for young flesh
an aphrodisiac,
inspiring priapism.

The gods like them young,
so the priests say.
"Death will strike your family
unless you bring a young virgin."

Prepubescent hymens
pierced by dark, quivering flesh,
shot at them like arrows.
Blood flowing out of tiny bodies
supporting an unbearable weight,
the weight of lust
with religious sanction.
The blood ceaselessly flows
like the Nile.

Never knowing
the carefreeness of youth.
Forced motherhood upon young bodies.
Enslaved by priests,
enslaved by families,
enslaved by their bodies.

IX

In North Africa today,
slaves, mostly female,
are still subjugated.
In Mauritania,
Tukoloi, Fulani and Wolof,
are enslaved by Arabs.
Illiterate women,
when asked if they're taken
against their will,
if they're raped,
don't understand the question.
They ask,
"Do you mean do the men come
to our tents at night?"

No need for
religious justification
and indoctrination.
"God created me to be a slave."
Drapetomania absent—
no desire to run away.
Where would they go?
They say,
"the masters are 'our people.'"

These nocturnal visits,
in West Africa,
in North Africa,
in the Americas,
spawned countless strains—
fifty-five.
These illicit
and even illegal visitations
from an alien race of men
continue to this day,
in huts,
in haute couture.
In some ways
we have become
more enlightened,
in others,
we are the same.

The past doesn't
really pass.

X

Not only Europeans,
but Arabs and Africans,
Muslims and Christians,
are culpable for the slave trade,
for selling black bodies.

They came under
the crescent.
Arabs descended upon
North and East Africa,
and Egypt,
enslaving Africans
in the name of Allah,
the Beneficent,
the Merciful.

They came under
the cross.
Europeans descended upon
West Africa,
enslaving Africans
in the name of Jesus,
Lord and Savior.

In West Africa
conquering tribe sold
the vanquished
to white men,
middle men in the middle passage.

From the coast
they brought the white slavers
into the interior,
"the dark continent,"
where "civilized" whites
went "native,"
revealing hearts of darkness.

Predators hunting human prey—
chattel.
Shackled, branded like cattle,
put into holding pens.
A babble of African languages
and dialects
screaming out in protest,
clanking chains providing
background noise.

Boarding ships,
put into the holds,
flesh upon flesh—
packed like sardines.
Lecherous white shipmen
sating their white bodies
on black flesh,
gold crucifixes swinging
from their necks
during these unholy unions.

"Ave Maria!"
they scream out in ecstasy,
profaning the name of Mary,
Mother of Jesus,
who was also taken
against her will,
as they rape black women,
some of whom would conceive
the first of many generations
of bastard "slaves"—
fifty-five strains.
Pardos.
They'd disembark
in the "New World"
with slavery's posterity
in their wombs.

XI

On the good ship Jesus,
their screams
were not heard by God.
Bloated bodies
would be regurgitated
on the shore,
signs of whippings visible.
And the sea would tell.

Something was begun
that couldn't be stopped,
at least not without
a declaration of war,
without fighting a bloody war.

A nation enriched by slavery,
fighting for its independence
against tyranny.
An eloquent spokesman said
that the price of liberty
may very well be death.
What was more eloquent
than slave women
bashing their newborns' heads
against rocks
to free them
from eternal bondage,
gray baby brain matter
fertilizing the soil.
And the land would tell.

William E. Waters

The founding fathers,
slave masters,
sanctioned slavery in the Constitution.
They were landowners,
men more concerned
with property than liberty,
one reason the Constitution
is rife with
contradictions
Slavery and freedom.
One nation.
Black and white.
Indivisible.
Separate and equal.
With liberty,
and justice
for all—
privileged white men.

XII

As the Nation prospered,
she was torn asunder.
Two nations.
One slave,
one free.
Two economies,
one agricultural,
one industrial.
The Confederacy,
the Union.
South.
North.

In the North,
in colonial New York City,
slaves were burned at the stake,
others were hanged
because of white fears
of a slave revolt,
of a "conspiracy"
to burn New York
and murder its inhabitants.

"Burn, baby, burn!"

White man, woman and
child must die.

Slavery was abolished
in Northern states.
Still, there was
uneasiness.
As long as there
were slave states,
whites couldn't trust blacks,
not even in free states.

In the North,
segregation was developed.
Blacks were ghettoized,
concentrated
in a few areas.
Revolts and
conspiracies
could be quickly
contained.

In the slave states:
Alabama, Arkansas, Delaware,
Florida, Georgia, Kentucky,
Louisiana, Maryland, Mississippi,
Missouri, the Carolinas,
Tennessee, Texas, and Virginia—
a roll call of infamy—
the land was most fertile,
as fertile as the wombs
of slave women
kept barefoot and pregnant
from white slave masters'
repeated rapes.

Black bodies
fertilized the soil,
a soil so red one could smell
the blood flowing where
the waterline began.
The land never wanted
for moisture,
as the blood, sweat and tears
of Africans
constantly rained upon it.

"This is my land, too,
I say, this is my land!"

XIII

On the land,
in the bloody fields,
one could hear
the deeply moving slave songs.
They helped slaves
make it through the day,
carrying an unbearable burden.
Slavery with religious sanction.
A God of love
transformed into
a God of hate.

Slaves singing gut-wrenching
spiritual lamentations
to the Lord of Hosts.
They were beyond spiritual;
they were painful
for God to hear.
But the masters weren't moved.
They articulated
a theology of slavery,
gave this peculiar institution
religious sanction.

"Slaves, obey your masters."
It is what God
commands you to do.
It's written
in the Good Book.

"God made me to be a slave."

Illiterate slaves had the Gospel
written upon their hearts
like the Ten Commandments
on stone tablets.
God did not call them
to be slaves,
to be beasts of burden.
Hadn't God once freed the Israelites
from bondage in Egypt?

Listen closely to the slave songs.
"Stealing away to Jesus."

Jesus!

Slaves never forgot that name.
Although white masters profaned it
to justify their trade
in black flesh,
there was a special appeal
to this name.

Jesus!

On the slave ships
the crew had referred to Jesus,
in more ways than one.
They screamed out Jesus' name
during rapes;
they talked about him
when they justified their trade.

They talked about how long
it would take Jesus
to arrive in the "New Word."
Slaves remembered that.
They calculated
the distance they traveled
by counting the stars
through cracks
in the holds of the ships—
knew that if Jesus was a way
to the New World,
then Jesus had to be
a way out,
out of the holds of ships,
across the dark waters,
back to Mother Africa.

"I am the way . . . ."

The good ship Jesus
would return them.

"Stealing away to Jesus."

They sang in the fields,
under the clear blue skies
and the red-rimmed watchful eyes
of jaded white overseers
who grinned at the slaves'
acceptance of Jesus,
who'd condemn them
to a lifetime of servitude.

"Slaves," I said, "obey your masters."

But the slaves were smiling,
not because they'd eat
pie in the sky;
they were envisioning
the good ship Jesus.

"Take me home, Oh! Lord, take me home."

"Stealing away to Jesus."

The singing rose to the heavens.
The sights on earth were hell.
There was everlasting shade
in heaven,
so they were told,
cool drinks on every cloud.
On earth there was so much cotton—
so much cotton to pick—
as far as the eye could see,
inducing a form of
snow blindness.
They rubbed their eyes
with raw, cotton pickin' fingers.

The scorching heat
turned the fields
into an Inferno.
Their parched lips
singing spirituals,
agonizing vowels
formed over cottonmouth.

"How long, Oh! Lord,
how long must
your people suffer?"

There was no Paradise on earth,
just the lie of pie in the sky.

Dreaming of pie in the sky,
the clouds transubstantiated
into whipped cream
on a thick slice
of sweet potato pie.

"Lord, just give me a piece
of dat pie 'fore I die!"

"No, give me liberty,
or give me death!
Not pie in the sky!"

From the very beginning
it was a system marked by death.

The stench of death
was everywhere.
Death during the raids
        on African land,
death during the trek
        from the interior,
death in the waiting pens,
death on the high seas,
death when they disembarked
        in the "New World,"
death when they defied
        the masters,
        a living death
        when slavery was their lot.

"God, I was not born
to be a slave."

"Give me liberty
or give me death!"

XIV

The seeds of rebellion
were sown in slavery's garden,
when Moses was first mentioned.
Even before his name was invoked.

"Pharaoh, let my people go!"

Slave women bruised
their pretty faces,
became frightening Medusas
to stone-cold stop the masters'
lust in its tracks.
When this didn't work,
some slave women
refused to wash,
became an abomination in smell
as well as sight.

The stench of death
was everywhere.

But nothing stopped
this white-hot lust
and white men brutally
raped black women,
again and again and again;
black women sometimes killed
the offspring.
It was a way to kill
the monsters,
the masters
of their bodies
who came to the cabins
in the darkness
to force themselves on them.
It was also a way to ensure
their unwanted children
did not live as slaves—
an act of kindness.

"Lord, I was not born
to be a slave,
nor my children."

XV

On the plantation,
there was no kindness.
There were no
happy-go-lucky slaves,
no sambos,
no Uncle Toms,
no Aunt Jemimas,
only in fiction,
where they seemed
to be treated kindly
by masters and mistresses.
The reality is that
slavery was brutal;
there were hundreds
of slave revolts,
mostly brutally suppressed.
Slaves burned at stakes.
Slaves hanged.
Slaves boiled alive
in big black kettles.

The price of liberty
was death.

The stench of death was everywhere.

Rebellion leaders
were Biblically inspired.
They saw their people
as Israelites in bondage
in Egypt.

"Pharaoh, let my people go!"

Slave masters' hearts
were stone-cold.
Rebellion leaders
sharpened their knives
on stones.
Under the starless nights
they planned.
White man, woman and child
must die.
No owner of slaves,
nor his family,
was innocent.
They all profited
by black labor in the fields.
Poor white trash
pretending to be gentility,
slaves at their beck and call
to fulfill their whims
and their fantasies.
White men
raping black women.
Black men providing
stud service
to white women.

The call to rebellion
was sounded on the drums—
a beat of immediacy.
It sounded like a heart
beating out of control,
ready to burst
with the effort.

In a surprise attack,
they'd slash and burn,
give burnt offerings
to the Biblical God
of vengeance.

"Burn, baby, burn!"

"Lord, their brutal enslavement
of your people
calls forth this judgment.
Let them be judged
for their iniquity,
and die for it.
Have no mercy on them."

The rebellions
were mercilessly suppressed,
hangings, beheadings,
burnings, whippings.
White fear transmogrified
into the brutality
history won't ever forget.
The Bards won't white-wash it.

The long shadow of history
overshadowing the present.

XVI

When Great God started
the works of creation,
there was a drumbeat.
When creation was completed,
there was a drum roll.

When Great God breathed
life into black bodies,
their heartbeats picked up
their rhythm from the drums.
When they took their first steps,
they seemed to be marching
to an internal drumbeat,
their hearts and feet synchronized.
It was a constant reminder
of the esteem
in which Great God
held drums.

The drumbeat could be heard
across time and space.
It conjured up images
of the Mother land,
of running free,
of dancing to the holy beat.
It was a sound
that had existed
in the beginning,
at the time of creation,
when Great God
played a drum roll.

William E. Waters

Slave masters outlawed drums;
they were instruments of rebellion.
White men knew that Africans,
and their descendants,
communicated in this language,
a language they hadn't lost,
since the beginning of time.

When white slave masters
heard the drums,
they remembered something
they never knew.
Slave traders had commented
how they'd heard this beat
when they stepped on African soil—
the pulse of a Nation.
When they raided African villages
with African slavers,
they heard this beat—
the heartbeat of a Nation.
When the Africans fled,
it sounded like a drum roll—
the rhythm of a Nation.

The drumbeat was ominous.
The slaves got restless;
instead of shuffling their feet,
they stepped lively,
so lively it seemed like a dance,
a danse macabre.
White man, woman and child
must die.
There were no innocents
in this inhuman trade.

The drumbeat was ominous.

There was foot-stomping:
the earth seemed to tremble.
Slaves danced around
and around and around,
in a frenzy.
They were remembering
when Great God gave them
the breath of life
and their hearts started
beating like drums.
They danced because
they remembered.
Their feet couldn't
stop moving.
They were not born
to be slaves.
They ran towards freedom.

XVII

Captured runaway slaves
had a foot chopped off.
Still, they ran on one foot.
When freedom called,
they ran.
Afflicted with drapetomania—
the impulse of a slave to seek freedom—
they ran.

They chased the North Star,
traveled by night.
Soon, there were established
routes, and stops.

There was a conductor
who'd never stop.
She was a statuesque figure,
called Moses by some,
Conductor by others.
She ran the Underground Railroad.

Slaves would get
on this midnight train,
wouldn't stop 'til
the break of dawn.

The bloodhounds were always
hot on their tails.
They'd been starved
and would be rewarded
with bloody meat
if they caught their prey.

The wind carried
the sound of barking dogs.
They were as mad
as their masters.
They salivated over
their sharp teeth,
which were filed,
which made them look
like vampires on four legs,
doggie dreams of feasting
on black flesh and blood
spurring them on.
When they were unleashed,
they picked up the scent
of black flesh, of fear;
they dashed into the woods.

The slaves were running scared.
If caught, they'd lose a foot.
They wouldn't be able
to dance anymore,
or walk with the same gait.
Great God had given them
dancing feet,
to step lively
to the drumbeat.

William E. Waters ❧ 51

They remembered
and picked up their pace,
'til their hearts beat louder
and the barking quieted.

When they made it
to the first stop,
they'd be safer.
They had to remain vigilant
'til they made it
to the Promised Land.

Stealing away at the midnight hour
on that midnight train from the slave states:
Alabama, Arkansas, Delaware,
Florida, Georgia, Kentucky,
Louisiana, Maryland, Mississippi,
Missouri, the Carolinas,
Tennessee, Texas and Virginia—
a roll call of infamy.

XVIII

Slave masters were poor sports.
They were playing
a brutal game,
a game in which
they couldn't tolerate losing.

They passed laws.
Runaway slaves
who'd made it
to a free state
were still slaves.
They could be returned
to the slave states.

Slaves ran farther North,
chasing the North Star.
Canada was
a place of refuge.
Since the Revolutionary War
ex-slaves had found
sanctuary there.

After the Fugitive Slave Act,
runaway slaves
ran even farther North.
It got colder,
but that was
the price of freedom.
They didn't shiver in the cold;
they remembered the heat
of the fields.

Slaves could be feverish
and delirious in the fields;
still, they had to toil—
no sick days.
Hot flashes ran
through their minds.
They could feel
the searing lash of the whips
on their backs.
Ugly scars criss-crossed
across their bodies.
One could read slavery's message
on their backs.
It was a sadistic institution,
maintained by whippings,
administered at
masters' and mistresses' pleasure.

Slaves who'd made it North
displayed their scars
before abolitionists
and sympathizers,
unveiling and revealing
slavery for what it was—
a brutal institution.

The scarring was grotesque.
Slavery was grotesque.
This evidence
of cruelty,
and barbarity,
shocked the conscience
of some,

inspired them
to fight slavery,
to fight against
man's inhumanity to man.

Slavery was a brutal institution,
its history written in blood,
sometimes on slaves' backs.
Slavery often resembled
a blood sport.
There was so much blood.

Slave masters were poor sports.
The rules favored them.
They couldn't lose;
they wouldn't accept losing
one slave.
The law was rigged
in their favor,
from the very beginning,
at the founding of the Nation,
written into the Constitution—
a corner stone—
and slave statutes
and black codes.
Slave masters lived
by these codes,
made their slave ownership
an inalienable right.
We hold these truths
to be self-evident . . .

XIX

For slave masters,
slavery was life itself,
the bread of life.
They feasted
off of black flesh
and off of the fruits
of free black labor.

A social as well
as an economic
way of life
developed.
It became addictive.

Slavery was a narcotic.
It anesthetized whites
against their inhumanity
and brutality.
In this state,
they justified their
trade in black flesh,
from pulpits,
in periodicals,
through pseudo-science.

They were addicted
to this way of life.
It fed their belief
in their superiority
and the slaves' inferiority.

Slaves weren't human;
they were chattel.
They were beasts of burden,
born to toil in the fields.
Since they were beasts,
they could be beaten
to keep them
in their place.

Slavery, a narcotic,
a drug in the bloodstream
of a Nation—
this blood running
through the
descendants of slave masters.

Recovering addicts,
recovering from slavery's
opium-like dream.
In denial,
denying the devastating
effects of slavery,
the continuing effects,
how we're haunted by
our history of slavery,
how the dark shadows of history
have been cast
across America,
how we live
in these shadows.

Only the truth
can set us free,
into the light of a new day,
out of the dark ages
of denial and distance.
For no matter how far
we distance ourselves
from slavery's history,
it's not too far from us.

Almost every encounter
in black and white
is haunted by
the specter of slavery.
There's white guilt,
and black shame.
There's white fear,
and black rage.
There's white anger,
and black hurt.
There's whitespeak,
and ebonics.

There's a world of difference
between black and white,
the Great Racial Divide,
an unspeakable chasm
technology cannot
build a bridge across.

XX

Slavery became
a political hot potato.
Manifest destiny
drove whites
to expand the Union.
Which new states would be slave,
which free?
Should the People decide this?
A line was drawn
in the red soil,
no expansion of slavery
beyond this point
in history.
Cross it and be prepared
to fight.

Bloody fighting broke out
in Kansas 'tween pro-slavery
"Border Ruffians"
and anti-slavery settlers
when the line was crossed.
The fighting began
and raged on.

John Brown's raid.
John Brown,
the real friend of the Negro.
Left out of the trinity
of "freedom fighters"
for black emancipation.

Denmark Vesey.
Nat Turner.
Gabriel Prosser.
Where is John Brown?

The Emancipator,
the Great Friend of the Negro,
the consummate politician,
said the South could have slavery,
but it couldn't break up the Union.
King Cotton thought otherwise.
The slave states
were the economic backbone
of the Union.
Damn Yankees!
This land was built
on the blood, sweat and tears
of free black labor.
Its continued prosperity's
based on free black labor.

Cotton as far
as the eye could see—
King Cotton reigned supreme

The Emancipator,
the Great Friend of the Negro,
wanted to relocate blacks.
Forcefully brought across
the high seas
to toil on the land,
now unwanted
after most of the work
had been done.

From the very inception
of the Nation,
this was a concern.
Could black and white
live together,
could they share the Nation?
Did they even have
the same dreams?

Blacks dreamed of freedom
and land to claim
as their own.
Forty acres.

Whites wanted slavery
and blacks to toil on the land.

In the War of Independence
the British had relocated blacks
who'd fought on its side
to Canada—the Promised Land.
After the Haitian Revolution,
"free blacks" fled to Haiti
in droves.
After Dred Scott—
a Supreme Court decree
expressing white sentiments:
blacks had no rights
that whites were bound to respect;
if they were born into slavery
they'd die slaves,
slavery everlasting—
more talk of emigrating.

There was no free soil
in the Union
on which they could stand,
not as freedmen and freedwomen.
They'd be brought back
to slave states
to toil on the land.
More plans to settle in Haiti.
There was a
"back to Africa" movement.
Blacks returned to Africa,
settled in Liberia,
and Sierra Leone.
The Nation wanted to annex
the Dominican Republic,
relocate blacks there.

Blacks wanted their freedom
and land to claim as their own.
At least forty acres,
why not throw in a mule?
They, as well as their ancestors,
fertilized this land
with their blood, sweat and tears.

"This is my land, too, I say,
this is my land!"

XXI

The Emancipator,
the Great Friend of the Negro,
wanted to save the Union,
at any cost.
The South could have slavery,
but it couldn't
break up the Union.

Southern disunionists.
Southern Secessionists.
The Confederate States of America.

The rebel states,
the Confederacy,
forced Abe's hand.
The Union was torn asunder.
Confederate cannons fired
on Fort Sumter.
Bloody fighting began.
It raged on.

At first blush,
redneck Southerners
had more to lose.
They fought with that passion
of people who believe
in what they're fighting for.
Northerners weren't
quite so passionate.
Were white men dying
so black men could be free?

William E. Waters   63

Draft riots in New York City.
White mobs attacking blacks,
willing to risk their lives
fighting black men
but not fighting white men
so black men could be free.

The Emancipation Proclamation
the Day of Jubilee!—
a shrewd political move.

The Day of Jubilee!—
Juneteenth.
Black feet dancing in the streets,
remembering the holy beat.
The balance of power
suddenly shifted.

The Northern cause
was infused with black passion.
Blacks in the slave states
were "freed" to fight
their former masters,
while the slaves in the
states loyal to the Union
remained slaves.

"Slaves in the Union,
obey your masters."

"Slaves in the Confederacy,
do *not* obey your masters."
Take up arms.
Fight for your freedom!
Liberty or death!

1st North Carolina Volunteers.
Corps d' Afrique.
54th Massachusetts Volunteer Infantry.
Marching to glory.

Blacks fought with the passion
of people who have everything
to lose, and gain.
They had to.
Redneck rebels would
kill back POWs—
no gentlemen rules of war—
that legendary southern
gentility absent—
not for black soldiers,
no Geneva convention.

One of white men's greatest fears
had come true.
Black men were facing
them across a battlefield,
the levelest of all playing fields.
Facing death.
Death, the great equalizer.
When black soldiers were captured,
they were killed.
The brutality against them
was inflicted with passion,
like crimes of passion,
destroying genitalia—
the big black cock
that had frightened white men
from the very beginning.

This treatment of black POWs,
of black soldiers,
was even more brutal
than the brutalest
treatment meted out
to the most recalcitrant slave.
These black soldiers
represented
the ultimate threat
to slave masters.
They'd set
a dangerous precedent.
They'd taken up arms.
They'd vowed
to kill white men,
slave masters
and their supporters,
for black freedom,
not to save the Union.
This outraged
white slave masters.

"How dare niggers
take up arms
against white men.
Abe was crazy
to arm niggers
in the first place,
to provide the seeds
for a future race war."

XXII

The South lost the war.
White Southerners were poor losers.
They shed their gray uniforms,
put on white robes,
went night riding,
fiery crosses
lighting the way.

After the War,
in the South,
blacks enjoyed
unprecedented political power,
along with scallywags
and carpetbaggers,
under the watchful eyes
of Northern troops.
This lasted for twelve years.
Blacks briefly experienced
the blessings
of liberty,
until the Great Compromise.

One more compromise
in a long line of compromises
compromising black freedom.

Written into the Constitution,
the Three-Fifths Compromise:
blacks, disenfranchised,
would be calculated
under this formula
for Southern white
political representation.

The Missouri Compromise—
Missouri, a slave state,
Maine, a free one;
no slavery in lands north
of Missouri's southern border.

The Compromise of 1850:
the problems of slavery,
pro and con,
just won't go away.

The Kansas-Nebraska Act:
a laissez faire approach
to slavery.

The Crittenden Compromise:
a proposed constitutional amendment,
allowing slavery
in all territories south of 36° 30'.

The Atlanta Compromise:
accept segregation,
develop useful skills,
harbor no resentment.

The Great Compromise—
the Hayes-Tilden Compromise:
picking a president.

Federal troops marched
out of Dixie.
States' rights won out,
slavery revisited.
Sharecropping, segregation
and peonage.

The Day of the Rope!

Night riders enforced the law.
Fiery crosses lit
up the skies.

Jesus crucified again,
burning on a cross.

All roads lead to the cross.

The cross
in white eyes,
symbolizing black slavery.

Fiery crosses.
"Burn, baby, burn!"

The cross,
in black eyes,
symbolizing freedom.

"I was not born
to be a slave."

Fiery crosses
burning.

"Burn, baby, burn!"

Bloody crosses
bleeding.

The blood of Christ
redeemed the world—
all one in Christ—
there's neither
Greek nor Jews,
slave nor freedmen.
Everyone is equal
at the cross.

XXIII

Exodusters.
Wagon trains of black people
heading West.

Go West, black man, go West.

Black men paved the way,
black women followed,
even mail order brides.

Go West, black woman, go West.

From Louisiana and Mississippi
blacks made the trek to Kansas,
Oklahoma and Nebraska.

Go West, black people, go west.

No manifest destiny here.
Seeking a new start,
leaving the bloody fields
and the fiery crosses
behind them.

Go West.

The Exodus West,
an arduous journey,
hostile whites, not Indians,
in the way.

William E. Waters ◄ 71

Go West.

This Exodus,
blacks in wagon trains,
never seen on TV,
a forgotten part of history,
like the black cowboys,
the history relegated
to the shadows.

Go West, black man, go West.
Go West, black woman, go West.
Go West, black people, go West.
Go West.
Go West.
Go West.

XXIV

The birth of a nation—
a white reign of terror
spread across the land.
Blood ran down the streets
as long as the Nile.
Redeemers and Red Shirts:
white supremacists
with black blood on their hands.
Hooded figures in white robes
with fiery crosses
in one hand,
nooses in the other.

"The Day of the Rope."

Black bodies swinging from trees:
strange fruit.

Cheering white mobs—
man, woman and child.
The new national pastime.

"Take me out to the lynching,
take me out to the tree . . . ."

Eenie, meenie, minie, moe,
catch a nigger by the toe,
if 'e 'ollers don't let 'im go,
string 'im up an' watch 'im choke.

Strange fruit,
swinging in the summer breeze.
Demure white ladies no longer
batted their eyes
or hid them behind fans.
Wide-eyed they watched their men
rid the black root
from sturdy tree trunk-like
ebony legs planted
firmly in American soil;
they rooted like cheerleaders.
Their eyes followed
the strange fruit
as their men
ripped it from the root
and threw it away,
discarded it like it was
something totally useless.

But it was like a boomerang.
It always came back at them,
in their dreams,
in their waking moments.

There was hysteria,
mostly imagined.
What if the big black buck
had his way with her?
Appalled that she was thinking
such thoughts,
but excited at the prospects,
even imagined,
she cheered the men on.

"Rip 'im apart!
Rip 'im apart!
Hang 'im!
Hang 'im high!

Her legs quivered,
her heart beat quickly,
but she'd not swoon.
Even if the big black buck
was innocent,
he had to think about it,
as she was thinking about it.
He deserved to be punished
for such thoughts.

She watched the strange fruit
swinging in the summer breeze.

This image haunted her dreams,
her sleepless nights.
The black hole in the center
of a once virile being—
no, a beast!
He was nothing but a beast,
a brute,
a savage.
Her man had the right idea.
Put the fear of God in him,
the fear of the cross.
Black brutes shall not trespass
upon her physical purity,
on her pure Christian thoughts.

The sign of the cross,
a fiery cross,
a bloody cross.
Black men hanging on crosses.
Strange fruit,
swinging in the summer breeze.

"Lord Jesus, white flesh is weak!
Save us from black flesh!"

She was tormented in her dreams.
She saw Jesus on a burning cross.
He was black.
He was missing his penis.
She remembered her
search for him,
in another time,
another place.
He'd been chopped up,
into fourteen pieces.
She'd found all
his body parts,
except his penis.
She put him back together,
helped him generate
a brand new penis.
When he was complete
once again,
she'd given herself to him.

It felt unreal,
like she was a disembodied spirit,
outside of herself,
watching a powerful black being
master her white body,
forcing cries of pleasure
from her.
This is what she lived for,
that part of her
that turned a blind eye
and a deaf ear
to her man's midnight
forays into the slave cabins.
She'd heard the screams,
she'd seen the children.
She knew it was wrong,
but she could not be moved.
Was this her punishment,
to dream of
"A black ram fucking a white ewe."
She was that ewe.

She screamed out,
awakened from her dreams.

She couldn't help
but get hysterical
when she saw a black man.
He haunted her dreams,
fucked with her subconscious.
He was an incubus.

He came to her those nights
she could sleep,
made her perform
unspeakable acts,
and enjoy them.
He was everything
she feared,
everything she hated.
He made her think
about her dream
about being a ewe,
about being fucked
by a big black ram.
He made her think
about the unthinkable.
He made her . . . .
He deserved to hang from trees.

"Hang 'im!
Hang 'im high!"

Strange fruit,
swinging in the summer breeze.

XXV

One Klan member
turned in his white robe
for a black one.
He sat on the Supreme Court.

Segregation was legalized,
became an institution,
just like slavery.
Blacks and whites were
even farther apart than
they were during slavery.
There was one great white line
dividing the nation—
the Great Racial Divide.
Neither back, nor white,
could cross it.
To do so would be to
incur the wrath of
segregationists and racialists,
to be labeled a "race traitor"
and a "nigger lover."

Blacks were separate,
considered equal—
the law turned upside-down.
Nothing could be shared
by the races—
toilets, transportation;
education, and eating facilities;
it was as if
blacks were contaminated,
would contaminate
everything they touched.
They were treated like lepers.
Blacks couldn't even share
the streets at the same time
as whites.
Had to step to the side,
across the great white divide,
bow their heads
and avoid eye contact.

One religion
worshipped in two churches.
Blacks, tired of the balcony,
had formed the true church,
everybody one in Christ.
But the body of Christ
was split in two.
Black and white,
separate and unequal.
A body of law supporting
segregated schools
and public facilities
sprang up like weeds.
They refused to be uprooted.
They were enforced with the rope.

"Hang 'im!
Hang 'im high!"
Old Man River
couldn't be crossed.
Like Proteus
he took on different shapes.
He was a trickster,
said you were separate
but equal;
relegated you to
substandard housing and schools
and said you were
separate but equal.
Old Man River
couldn't be crossed.

XXVI

Black Summer.
White women.
Enraged white mobs
stormed into black quarters
with murderous intent.

A black beast,
a goddamn jigaboo,
a coon,
a nigger,
an ape,
a savage,
a brute,
a sexual predator,
raped a white woman.

Hysterical white women
pulled their hair
as they remembered
their dreams.
The big black ram
was unfettered
and seeking them out.
They'd be raped like
that poor woman.
These black beasts
had to be stopped!

The "news" traveled quickly.
Chivalrous white men,
always on twenty-four hour call
to protect white womanhood,
took their nooses out of drawers.

"The Day of the Rope."

Like locusts
they swarmed into black areas
with murderous intent,
looking for the sexually
deranged black brute—
and they were all
sexually deranged and brutes—
who'd offended the white race,
who'd dared to
step across the great divide
and take unwanted liberties
with a white woman.

"Mary, mother of God,
no such crime
shall go unpunished!"

Innocent black men,
and they were mostly innocent,
were trussed up like cattle.
They were beaten;
they were burned;
they were castrated;
they were hanged.

"Hang 'em!
Hang 'em high!"
white women screamed
at the top of their lungs.

"Send 'em to Nigger Heaven."

At the same time,
there was a renaissance,
the Harlem Renaissance.

From pickin' cotton
        to the Cotton Club.
"Nigger Heaven" discovered.

The old beat translated,
put into music
to dance to,
and poetry—
"If We Must Die."

The Harlem Renaissance,
time of hope,
time of possibilities.

The Roarin' 20s.
Hoodlums and molls
and flappers.
Thrill-seeking
and curious whites
journeyed to Harlem,
discovered "Nigger Heaven."

But most of the white world
was in the dark.
They'd never journeyed out
of the heart of whiteness,
out of segregated
white strongholds.
They saw nothing wrong
with "going native,"
despite proclamations
of civilization,
and southern gentility.
They yelled and screamed
their tribes' war cry.
Like cowboys they twirled
their ropes in the air,
caught black men in them,
trussed them like cattle,
hoisted them up on trees.

"Hang 'em
Hang 'em high!"

Strange fruit,
swinging in the summer freeze.

Before the hangings,
they cut pieces of black flesh,
fed them to their dogs—
their best friends—
kept some as keepsakes.
They put their hands
on their hearts,
watched the cross burning,
watched the nigger swinging.

William E. Waters

Strange fruit,
swinging in the summer breeze.

Swing high,
swing low,
coming for to carry
me home.

Broken necks,
broken bodies.
Black souls
ascending to "Nigger Heaven"—
another place of segregation.

This was a lesson
to all nigger boys and men.
They were not free
to rape white women.
They'd hang them
as quickly as they'd
look at them.
If they even looked
at a Christian white woman,
they'd go to "Nigger Heaven."

They'd see
our Lord and Savior
Jesus Christ
on a fiery cross.

"Burn, baby, burn!"

They'd burn in hell
with that image
burned on their flesh
and seared on their minds.

XXVII

Out of the African Diaspora
an idea emerged.
"Africa for Africans"—
Pan-Africanism.
A would-be black emperor.
An idea to deal with
"the tragedy of white injustice."
A star ship line to transport
black bodies and
black-produced goods.
To sail the high seas,
to return to Mother Africa
as freedmen and freedwomen,
some a generation
removed from slavery.

Painful ancestral memories,
of clanking chains,
and screaming women.
At every port of call,
multicolored descendants
of Africans present—
the African Diaspora.
They spoke different tongues,
as they had
when they were kidnapped
from Mother Africa.
Now they were the languages
of their former slave masters.

Linguistic differences,
a multitude of evolved
cultural differences—
the tribes hardly
recognized each other.
But the similarities
were striking.
There was one source,
one root—
Mother Africa—
the root Redeemers and Red Shirts
and Klansmen
were trying to extirpate.
The root was now firmly
planted in foreign soil.

"These are my lands, too,
I say, these are my lands."

The blood, sweat and tears
of Africans
and their descendants
fertilized these lands.

Though transplanted,
the connection was there.
Africa called some.
Was it atavism—
the call of the ancestors:
The collective unconscious.

The would-be black emperor declared,
"Africa for Africans!"

The journey across the Atlantic.
The ocean floor's littered
with African skeletons.
Sharks had been fattened
from so man dark bodies
jettisoned into the deep—
human cargo turned into
flotsam and jetsam—
part of the refuse
of the triangular trade.

A powerful idea,
Pan Africanism,
never found its roots,
scattered like the nations,
like the bones
on the ocean's floor—
a most precious resource,
humans,
on the ocean's floor
like buried treasure.

Pan Africanism,
a treasure waiting
to be rediscovered.

XXVIII

The Great Migration.
The Second Exodus
out of the South,
a land far crueler
to Africans and their descendants
than Egypt ever was
to the Biblical Israelites.

"Pharaoh, let my People go!"

From the Southern fields
      to the Northern factories,
black labor transplanted.
In search of a better life.
The Promised Land.

The wilderness
mistaken for the Promised Land.
At first,
their prospects seemed better.
But there was no land.
There was nothing more important
than land.
One could live
off the fat of the land.

Tenements replaced shacks.
Packed in apartments
like sardines,
reminiscent of the
holds of save ships.
The asphalt jungle.

There was nowhere
to plant gardens.
A rural people,
an agrarian people,
suddenly urbanized,
industrialized.

From the fields
to the factories,
black labor transplanted.

From pickin' cotton
        to assembly lines,
From Mississippi
        to the Motor City.
From Chattanooga
        to the Windy City.
From cash crops
        to shooting craps.

Tossed to and fro
by winds of fortune.

The Great Migration,
the Second Exodus
out of the South,
looking for the Promised Land,
a land of milk and honey,
streets paved with gold.
Another white lie.
Segregation had developed
up North.
Chasing this dream.
Faced with an American dilemma:
a dream for some,
a nightmare for others.
Two nations,
one black,
one white,
separate and unequal.

XXIX

From Civil War
      to Civil Rights.
All that'd been won
was lost and was
being fought for again.

Slavery ended,
sharecropping and
segregation began.
Civil rights were granted,
they were ignored.
Given the franchise,
not allowed to vote—
intimidation at the polls.
Grandfather clauses.
Poll taxes.

National Guards replaced
federal troops.
States' rights enforced.

White Citizens' Councils.
Segregationists.

King Cotton metamorphosed
into a crow—
Jim Crow,
the new overseer.

Looking to the Law,
an alabaster bitch
with a blindfold on her eyes,
peeking underneath it.
She has a heart of stone.
She shall not be moved.

Decades of litigation,
from *Plessy* to *Brown*,
chipping away at
the stones of law,
of legal segregation,
of this alabaster bitch
on a pedestal.
She's a symbol,
of justice denied.
The overseer
of segregation.

Little black children
indoctrinated
in segregated schools
on Flag Day,
pledging allegiance
to an indivisible nation
under God,
with a promise
of liberty
and justice,
for all.

Hallowed truths ring
hollow in the ears
of these children.
Two nations,
one black, one white,
separate and unequal.

"Whites only!"
"Colored."

Jim Crow overseeing
segregated
toilets;
transportation;
schools;
churches;
restaurants;
even prisons.

Segregation.
Jim Crow
cawing loudly
perched on Justice's shoulder,
a white bitch
with a heart of stone.

XXX

The drumbeat
could still be heard—
the heartbeat of a nation.
There was a different
drum major,
but he was playing
the same beat
that Great God had played
at the beginning of creation,
that men and women
are born free.

From Montgomery
        to Memphis.

Marching feet
and singing voices.
The dream:
"We shall overcome."

Tired black women
walked miles to work—
the long walk home—
wouldn't ride
in the back of the bus.
Brown-bagging lunch
to avoid segregated
lunch counters.

Jim Crow
could have his buses,
ride his buses
by his lonesome,
eat lunch alone.

Empty buses,
emptying pockets.
tired black women,
their footprints in the dust,
trekking to work.
The long walk home.

One last desperate rally.
The dogs were unleashed;
they hadn't tasted
black flesh and blood
in years.
They howled like
hungry werewolves.

They wanted black flesh.
They salivated,
remembering their
classical conditioning.
On long leashes,
they attacked their human prey.
Trained by their masters
to attack blacks,
dogs trained to be
discriminating.
A new breed:
racist attack dogs.

Angry white mobs
beating up
peaceful black protesters.
Anger permanently etched
on white faces:
man, woman and child.

"Smile, you're on candid camera."

The American dream—
a waking nightmare
for blacks.

Nothing sacred.
Sixteenth Street Baptist Church.
Four little black girls
bombed in a church
by Klansmen.

"Where are you, O Lord,
in your people's time of need?"

Domestic terrorism
perpetrated by whites
against blacks.
Sanctioned by law,
enforced by politicians.

A black teenage boy
beaten to death
for "sassing" a white woman.
An open coffin
for the while world to see.

"Look what they did to
my boy!"

America in all her
uncivilized glory.

The world watched,
and was horrified.
The defender of democracy,
an evil empire in disguise.
It'd gotten fat
off of free black labor.
It couldn't come to grips
with its high-sounding
rhetoric.
One nation.
Indivisible.
With liberty.
And justice.
For all . . .
white people.

This had to be
the demonic at work.

A black prince named this evil.

"Devils!
Blond-haired.
Blue-eyed.
White devils!"

A nation within a nation.
Proud clean-shaven black men
in business suits
and bow ties.

Veiled black women,
long flowing dresses
concealing their
voluptuousness
from lecherous
blue eyes.

From naked on the
auction block
      to veiled and modestly
      attired in the mosque.
Black womanhood honored,
protected from
lustful white men
who'd had their way
with them
for hundreds of years,
bastardizing the race.

Beautiful sisters,
the fifty-five strains
conceived in rape
represented.
Their womanhood restored.
Proud black men
ready to defend
and protect them.

A black Nation,
not fighting to integrate.
Seeking reparations,
some land,
some states
to call our own.

The blood, sweat and
tears of Africans,
and their descendants,
fertilized this land.
We have a claim
on this land.
We have a right to it.

We'd gladly separate.
We don't need you.
We don't want to live
among you.
We just want to be
separate and equal.
This was called,
"The hate that hate produced."

The Nation
that hate produced.

The Nation of Islam—
Black man, woman
and child—
the sun, the moon,
a star.

The Nation.
Proud clean-shaven black men
in business suits
and bow ties
Veiled black women
in long flowing dresses.

XXXI

JFK called upon
to enforce the law,
to send federal troops
back into Dixie.

A student of history,
beholden to the Dixiecrats,
a copperhead of sorts,
this Yankee Doodle Dandy.
This King Arthur of the 60s
had no Merlin at Camelot
to call upon.
He sat in the Oval Office
like it was a commode,
wouldn't shit
or get off the pot.

Federal troops
had departed from the South
because of the Great Compromise,
gave the North
a president in return.
The South erected
legal segregation,
sanctioned by the High Court.
JFK lives
in the shadows of this history.
The thought of

Federal troops on Southern soil
rekindled memories
of the Civil War,
of the South's defeat,
of Reconstruction,
of Radical Republicans,
of carpetbaggers
and scalawags.

Slums on the outskirts
of the White House.
Could be Brazilian *favelas*—
hovels on the outskirts,
in the shadows
of grand structures,
monuments to democracy
and capitalism
and racism.
A tale of two cities.
A second Civil War's
brewing.

Southerners sill fly
the confederate flag,
mocking the Union,
insulting their black citizens.
Dixie's keen on states' rights,
a laissez faire approach
to the "race problem."

"Now don't ya'll
Northerners come down
'ere stirrin' up
our Negroes."

"Agitators!"
"Troublemakers!"

The last time
Northerners went South,
they took over,
set themselves up in power,
uplifted blacks,
gave them political power.

Blacks,
disenfranchised
as soon as federal troops
started marching North.
Dixiecrats in power
in both houses,
have a stranglehold
on the White House

JFK,
no Abe Lincoln,
backed down
from Southern politicos
let them stand
in the way of racial progress,
let them enforce
Southern justice.

The best JFK could do
was appoint a black lawyer
Solicitor General.
A profile in courage,
this man with
no measure of magic,
no Merlin at Camelot.
A politician,
pure and simple,
no Radical Republican,
a New Frontier Democrat
working within
the same borders,
the same racial constructs.
Now, part of American mythology,
a time that never existed.

XXXII

Freedom Summer.
Free white women.
Freedom voter campaigns.
Freedom rides.
Free love.
Interracial liaisons.
Between black males/white females.
Jungle fever.
Talking black,
sleeping white.

Black women resentment.
Narcissistic white women,
putting their desires
ahead of the Movement.

As slave mistresses,
as abolitionists,
as suffragettes,
as feminists,
as civil rights sympathizers,
white women
put their desires first.
Slavery, one said,
degraded white men
more than Negroes.
For the vote,
they appealed to
white supremacy
at the polls.

Appalled that white men
had given black men
the vote over white women,
they showed their true color—
lily white supremacists.
As feminists,
they appealed to class,
their privileged status
as white women,
not their sex,
which would've included black women.
As civil rights sympathizers,
they looked to their desires,
their personal fulfillment.
These Eves would taste
the forbidden fruit,
even if they destroyed
the movement in the process,
and a few good black men.

White bitches,
hair like horses' manes.
She could take one,
hang her from her hair,
beat the privilege out of her first.
Thought she could take black men
away from black women,
parade her forbidden whiteness
before them
and they'd break out in a fever,
a severe case of jungle fever.

Black males/white females.
Jungle fever.
Talking black,
sleeping white.

From the beginning of time,
white women
sat on their privilege,
used it to their advantage.
They never owned up
to false accusations of rape.
They sat there,
watched the burning crosses,
cheered as black men
danced on the ends of ropes—
the *danse macabre americain*.

For every innocent black man,
there were ten guilty white females.
For every guilty black male,
there were ten false accusations.
They could get all hysterical,
Oscar-acting the part,
their straw-colored hair mussed
from their own fingers.
They could scream at
the top of their lungs,
their screams a siren song,
bringing black men to destruction,
singing lying arias.
Black women know.

Strange fruit,
swinging in the summer breeze.

The Scottsboro Nine
and countless others.
Black women know.

There was so much resentment,
competing for black men,
their whiteness a distinct
advantage.
Competing with this
coveted image,
this ideal,
long blond hair,
blue eyes,
fair skin,
aquiline nose,
thin lips,
big breasts,
long legs,
no ass so speak about.
Still, it was a standard of beauty,
a standard they could never
quite measure up to,
not with hair straighteners,
not with skin lighteners,
not with pinching their noses
(not with contact lenses,
not with cosmetic surgery—
liposuction,
rhinoplasty,
breast reduction,
tummy tucks)—
not with high heels,
not with dieting.
Black women know.

William E. Waters

There was this fatal attraction,
and a fatal rejection.
What did her man see in her?
She was a selfish,
calculating white bitch.
This Pandora had
let lynching out of the box;
she only brought misery,
pain and suffering.
Black men were destroyed
because of screaming, hysterical
and lying white women.
They had this power
to destroy black men.
Was that the attraction?
That men love the thing
which can destroy them?
Was the black man bent
on his own destruction?
In all things,
she would have
the upper hand.
Why place your black self
in her white hands?
She was a cold white bitch
who'd castrate you
as quickly as she'd look at you.
What was this fatal attraction
all about?
Black women don't know.

Freedom summer.
Free white women.
"Free love"
at a terrible price.
Black males/white females.
Jungle fever.

"Burn, baby, burn!"

XXXIII

Barking dogs
chased peaceful protesters.
Children water-hosed
down in the streets,
a cruel summer sport.

"Nigger, nigger, nigger!"

Angry white mobs,
a spectator sport
of jeering and
spitting and cursing
black people.

"Nigger, nigger, nigger!"

Red faces.
Rednecks.
White fists flying,
meeting black flesh.
Nonviolent/violent confrontations.

"Nigger, nigger, nigger!"

White rage.
Red-hot white rage.
Thin chapped lips,
blistered,
blistering imprecations.

"Nigger, nigger, nigger!"

The Second Civil War,
the race question unresolved,
unresolvable in the face of this
jeering and spitting and cursing.

"Nigger, nigger, nigger!"

XXXIV

Black Panthers.
Black power.
Black theology.
Black is beautiful!

"Say it loud:
'I'm black and I'm proud!'"

The shuffling stopped,
bowed heads were lifted.
The holy beat
was remembered,
incorporated into
James Brown's hits.
They marched in the streets.
They sang in the streets.

Lift every voice and sign:
"Say it loud:
'I'm black and I'm proud!'"

Panthers patrolled the streets,
berets on heads,
rifles in hands.
Revolutionary chic.
The Revolution
was being televised.

A big black fist
was poised at white America,
ready to strike back
after all these years
of nonviolent/violent confrontations.

On the streets,
kids sang:
Ungawa!
Black Power.
Destroy.
White boy.
I said it.
I meant it.
I'm here
to represent it.
I'm cool.
I'm calm.
I'm soul brother
number nine.
sock it
to 'em
one mo' time.
Ungawa!

They danced
around and around
in a frenzy.
Understanding
complicated truths
reduced to slogans.

Ungawa!

Their little faces,
dead serious.
Kill,
or be killed.

Ungawa!

Black Power
was a force.
It even gave kids
a sense of power.
The power
to dream
of killing.

White man, woman
and child must die.

Ungawa!

XXXV

Armed panthers
readied their guns.
We also hold these truths
to be self-evident:
that we have the right
to bear arms,
and to use them.

The Black Panther Party
for Self Defense.

"Shoot the mad dogs down
in the streets!"

"Shoot the racist pigs down
in the streets!"

One panther,
whose soul was on ice,
fired up white America,
declared that the rape of
white women
by black men
was a revolutionary act.
(Years later, in
That's Blaxploitation,
there's "The Blackman's
Guide to Seducing White Women
With the Amazing
Power of Voodoo.")

White males' greatest fear,
that black men
would do to white women
what white men
had done to black women—
that black men
would rape white women,
was realized,
at least in print.
What they'd suspected
all along
was finally in black and white
for the whole world to see.
"See, the nigger is
a beast,
a brute,
a sexually deranged animal
who'd trample upon
white womanhood
if given half the opportunity."

The war against
the Black Panthers
intensified.
White men were
properly motivated.
Nothing got them up
like the prospect of
protecting white womanhood
from black satyrs,
from big black bucks,
from these sinister sexual superstuds.

If niggers had their way,
if Black Power
was realized,
there'd be
a Black House.
They'd hold
interracial orgies
in the Black House.
No white woman
would be safe
from these
highly sexed animals
with big cocks.
They were nothing more
than penises personified,
waiting to pounce
on white women,
if given half the opportunity.
They must be emasculated.
The root must be uprooted.

Othello.
Bigger Thomas.
Joe Christmas.
Emmett Till.
Willie Horton.
Central Park Attackers.
Rodney King.
Nushawn Williams.
Big, bad black bogeymen.

An age-old tale,
of sexual jealousy,
of the power of the penis,
the power black Priapus
has over white minds.
And we thought this
was about civil rights.

XXXVI

COINTELPRO
Counterintelligence—
the Program.
Get with it.
Destabilization
in the black community,
among the black leadership,
within civil rights,
and militant groups—
the plan.
Set them against each other.
Plant dissension.
Watch it bloom
through careful cultivation.
Undermine them through
misinformation.

Judases enlisted.
They come
a dime a dozen.
Brainwashed from day one.
"I pledge allegiance
to the Flag,
and to the
Federal Black Inquisition."

Betrayal upon betrayal.
From slave rebellion
        to civil rights
        to black power.

The good Negroes,
counterrevolutionaries,
counting the baubles
they're given,
for selling out.

For selling out
Prosser and Turner
and Vesey and Brown.
For selling out Martin
and Malcolm
and the Panthers.
For selling out the race.

The question of race
just won't go away.
Living in the shadows
of it.

XXXVII

The Black prince
is felled
by one of his own.
Proud black men,
clean-shaven,
in business suits
and bow ties,
turned envious.
Misinformation took root.
Fanatics.
Fools.
Unwitting tools
of the oppressors.

The black prince.
Gunned down
in front of
his wife and children.
She cradles his head,
a real profile in courage.
The children watch,
two more in mother's womb,
crying for the father
they'd never see alive,
only brought to life
by memories,
by faded pictures,
by movies.

Canonized.
Sanitized.
Commercialized.
Buy an X hat,
or tee shirt.
Remember the man
as he wasn't.

"Too black!
Too strong!"

XXXVIII

"The King is dead!
Long live the King!"

From Montgomery to Memphis.
On the Lorraine Motel balcony,
a bullet found its mark.
He was marked for death,
from the very beginning,
when he challenged
the sacred crow
of segregation.
A redneck racist behind a rifle,
put the king in his sights,
while white G-men watched.
"They always get their man."

Decades later,
evil white men gloated
in the White House,
called the King
"Martin Lucifer Coon."
These devils demonizing
the late Prince of Peace,
part of the white backlash,
against Reconstruction,
against Civil Rights,
against Black Power,
against affirmative action.

Angry white men
rule the world.

Even the Prince of Peace
had his Judas,
a "kiss-and-tell" autobiographer.
Live a grave robber,
he unearthed half-truths
and FBI misinformation.
Fed into the stereotype,
of the oversexed black male.
Like Osiris,
a postmortem
castration by his brother.

But King's Judas
was cursed.
He was struck down,
like some awful Egyptian curse
had been set in motion
by his betrayal,
by unearthing half-truths
and FBI misinformation.

"The King is dead!
Long live the King!"

Conspiracy theories abound.
Was the convicted killer
the killer?
Or did the G-men
really get their man?

A black rage
consuming itself.
Fire destroying areas,
never to be rebuilt.
The price of rage,
and revolution.

"Burn, baby, burn!"

XXXIX

Young black panthers
hunted down in the streets
by the FBI:
Federal Black Inquisitors.

"Shoot first!
No questions later."
(This policy's been handed down,
to New York's Finest,
to the LAPD—
famous for *Dragnet*,
an unofficial license
for police to stop and search
anyone who looked
"vaguely suspicious";
black men fit this bill;
they all looked alike—
to New Orleans cops,
and other police departments
across the nation
whose officers have a predilection
to shoot unarmed
black men and boys,
even a kid
with a candy bar
with silver wrapping,
mistaken for a gun.)

Gunned down
in cold blood.
G-men pat themselves
on the back.
"They always get their man."

This militant group,
a threat
to the internal insecurity
of the nation,
a threat
to white hegemony,
and white superiority,
a threat
to white supremacy,
a threat
to the self-evident truths
by which the nation
was conceived.

"We hold these truths
to be self-evident . . .
that all white men
are superior to black men;
that black men have no rights
that white men are bound to respect."

XL

War was declared,
on two fronts:
at home and abroad.
As American troops fought
to make the world
safe for democracy,
or to end all wars,
or to stop communism
from spreading
like a communicable disease,
she was fighting
a domestic war.

From the War for Independence
        to the Vietnam War,
from sea to shining sea,
blacks fought for American ideals,
the ideals America preached
to the world abroad
but didn't practice at home—
not for her
black citizenry.

Reluctantly recruited
throughout history—
even during slavery:
the slave enlistment bill—
oftentimes volunteering:
the War of 1812—

America now called upon
her able-bodied black men
to fight people of color.
Put them on the front lines.
It didn't matter
that they had nothing to gain
in a separate and unequal world,
their lives to lose.

The Greatest
eloquently stated:
"People call me nigger
in this country
every day."
It was reported as:
"No Vietcong ever
called me nigger."

"Nigger, Nigger, nigger!"

Those are fighting words!
If there's fighting to be done,
America's a good place
to start.

Uncle Sam wants you!
A white finger
pointing at a
black male—
Selective Service.

If the Greatest
wouldn't fight abroad,
he wouldn't fight at home.

Stripped of his license to fight,
this heavyweight champ,
he fought his battle in court,
won years later.
But Uncle Sam had called,
and if Uncle Sam wants you,
he gets you,
one way or another.
Uncle Sam
always gets his man.

Now, we canonize
the defiant black man
who threw his Olympic gold medal
in the river.
He was great for doing that.
He was great for not
fighting in a war
he didn't believe in,
against people who'd
never called him nigger.

"Nigger, Nigger, nigger!"

Those are fighting words.
If there's fighting
to be done,
America's a good place
to start.

We canonize him—
the Greatest—
for the wrong reasons.

XLI

Opposition to the war.
Something unusual for
red, white and blue Americans—
as hawkish as they come.
America had fought
war after war after war
with very little
internal opposition.
That's un-American.
There was nothing like this
in recent memory.

It wasn't long before
a soulful singer sang,
"Bring the boys home,
bring them back alive."

The Prince of Peace
had opposed this war.
It was morally wrong.
It was an unjust war.
(The hawks
kept an eye on him.)

Justification for
the war
was manufactured.
Perhaps no one understood
what was at stake,
what we were fighting for.
But the fighting raged on.

"Bring the boys home,
bring them back alive."

Body bags returned
in record numbers
with young men—
among them
the youngest veterans
of all our wars—
whose lives were snuffed out
in the summer
of their youth,
in rice paddies and jungles
halfway across the world.

"Bring the boys home,
bring them back alive."

Black men,
scorned at home,
denied basic rights
and human dignity,
called upon
to fight abroad,
halfway across the world,
to fight
for American ideals,
while their white counterparts
evaded the draft,
used white privilege
to exempt themselves;
their black counterparts
at home
were gunned down
in the streets by
Federal Black Inquisitors,
while angry whites
shouted and screamed and jeered:
"Nigger, nigger, nigger!"

"No Vietcong ever
called me nigger."
Those are fighting words.
If there's fighting
to be done,
American's a good place
to start.

Veteran hospitals
filled up,
along with mental hospitals.
An old syndrome renamed—
the brutality of war
was taking its toll
on young minds.
They'd seen too much
in rice paddies
and jungles
halfway across the world.

The fighting raged on.

The passion couldn't be
maintained for this war.
What was really at stake
but the hearts and minds
of our troops,
of our national conscience.

Betrayal,
not a distant memory.
The slave enlistment bill
during the Revolutionary War
conscripted slaves
to fight
for their masters' freedom.
Still enslaved
after the War for Independence.

Still landless
after the War of 1812,
despite General Andrew Jackson's
(later President),
promise to give tracts of land
to every black man
who joined his army
of irregulars
to fight the British.
They signed up in droves,
distinguished themselves,
only to be betrayed.
A recurrent theme in
American history
vis-a-vis blacks and whites.
Betrayal upon betrayal
upon betrayal—
broken promises.

After the Civil War
and the Reconstruction years,
blacks were quickly disenfranchised—
sharecropping and peonage
replaced slavery.
After the Spanish-American war,
awarded a rope
to put around their necks—
the white man
placed ropes
around black necks—
the Nigger Medal of Dishonor.

After World War I,
despite a scholar's
insistence
that fighting this war
was also a fight
for their place
in American society—
they returned
to a Black Summer,
lynchings and race riots.
After World War II,
returned to have Jim Crow
severely circumscribing
their lives.
They were separate but equal—
one of those
American white lies.
The same,
after the Korean War
And then the Vietnam War,
a protracted war
that became unpopular,
they returned to
a nation divided,
to drugs and despair,
to mental hospitals
and prisons.

"Bring the boys home,
bring them back alive."

Journeying into
the heart of darkness.
"Apocalypse Now!"
Agent orange.
Forests on fire.
"Burn, baby, burn!"
Land mines exploding.
Peasants waging
a war against
American invaders.
Death everywhere.

The Vietnam War,
a partial success.
It defeated the
Civil Rights
and Black Power movements.
At home,
and abroad,
the black male vanguard
was killed,
co-opted,
marginalized,
narcotized
or imprisoned.

XLII

Meanwhile,
on the home front,
the black body count increased,
as panthers were gunned down
in the streets.
Even white allies were given
a taste of ugly white
Mississippi racism,
which demands that
they choose sides—
white is right.
Get with the Program,
or else.

"Mississippi Burning."
"The Long Walk Home."
"Clara's Heart."

Camelot mythologized
even more,
creating other myths:
the FBI actively
involved in enforcing
civil rights laws;
whites in leading roles
in the Civil Rights
Movement.

The reality:
the FBI watched
white racists terrorize
blacks and their white allies;
the FBI even actively
disrupted the Movement;
angry whites,
yelling and screaming and jeering:
"Race traitor!"
"Nigger lover!"
"Nigger, nigger, nigger!"

Up against this hate.
Death was everywhere.

The president was dead.
The King was dead.
The prince was dead.
The president's brother was dead.
Civil Rights workers were dead.
The young panthers were dead.

Up against this hate.
Death was everywhere.

The aftermath of civil war.
Smoldering ruins in ghettoes.

"Burn, baby, burn!"

Rage still burning
in black hearts and minds
long after the fires
had been extinguished.

The 60s—
the Decisive Decade—
ideally challenged white America,
to be better,
to live up to
her high-sounding ideals.

The 60s—
its legacy:
the death of a generation,
of the future,
of a better America.

XLIII

No phoenixes rose
from the ashes
of the deaths
of the 60s.

The Black Liberation Army
tried urban guerrilla warfare.
They were outnumbered,
they were outgunned.

Black male revolutionaries,
white women on their arms.
Talking black,
sleeping white.
Revolutionary chic.
Berets.
Tight black leather outfits—
something sexually suggestive
about this.
Paramilitary uniforms—
something tragicomic
about this.
Dashikis—
something unreal
about this.
African garb—
reclaiming what's lost forever.

William E. Waters

From the big house
        to safe houses.
From auction blocks
        to robbing banks.

America pulled them apart
only to bring them together.

A rebellious heiress.
Was she brainwashed,
or put under a spell?
Black magic?
"The Blackman's Guide
to Seducing White Women
with the Amazing Power of Voodoo."

She had to be
under a spell,
under an insidious
black influence—
voodoo!

There was always
an enormous social price
she'd have to pay,
for intimacy,
or even sympathy,
with black males.

But she could always return,
a prodigal daughter,
an Eve who'd tasted
the forbidden fruit,
wiser for the experience.

This descendant of Eve
never lost
her inquisitiveness,
the desire to know
both good and evil.
The forbidden beckoned her,
seduced her.
She'd tasted
the forbidden fruit,
and lost her innocence
but became wiser.

Still, she could always return,
a prodigal daughter,
turn in her gun,
turn her back
on the revolution,
and become "respectable"
once again,
while her black male
compatriots and lovers
rotted in jail.

She could flirt
with black revolutionaries,
fuck them with a vengeance,
accept their anger,
mistake it for passion,
for an uncontrollable
desire for white flesh.
Jungle fever—
she could see him
swinging from her hair.

She could see herself
tied to a tree.
She could see him
beating his chest,
stripping her
and punishing her
for the desire
she inspired.

She could burn her bra,
denounce the war in Nam,
and later be transformed
into a super-capitalist,
even marry a billionaire.
She could always return,
a prodigal daughter.

She'd rebelled.
She was wiser
for the experience.
No one could ever
accuse her of not
following her heart's desire,
even if it had led her
to a place she'd been
forbidden for centuries.

She could always return.

XLIV

He could never return,
a man so far removed
from his ancestral homeland,
roots planted firmly
in American soil,
soil fertilized with the
blood, sweat and tears
of black folk.

The gift of sweat and brawn.

He could never forget,
the enslavement
of his ancestors,
especially
the rapes of the women,
as he impotently watched,
his head bowed in shame,
forced to be a father
to the rapists' "children,"
later tagged as
irresponsible,
an absentee father.
He'd been a father
to the masters' progeny
for hundreds of years.
Lest we forget.

Consumed by a black rage
that blinded him,
and revenge,
he lost sight
of the prize.

From war to revolution,
he'd tried his hand.
The Establishment
sought his amalgamation—
the ongoing myth
of the melting pot.
E pluribus unum.
The bottom line:
be more like us
and all of this shall
be yours.
"We'll even give you
a white woman
if you behave."

The last temptation.
Judases with their hands
out for silver pieces.

Confused.
Searching for identity.
Fifty-five strains.

Pardos.

Mestizo;
quinteron de mestizo;
requinteron de mestizo;
blanco.

Mulatto;
quadroon or quadroon of mulatto;
quinteron de mulatto or octoroon;
requinteron de mulatto.

Mulatto;
zambo, sambo or lobo;
cuateron or quadroon.

Coyote.

Cambuja;
sambahiga;
calpamulatto or chino;
givero.

Creoles;
caboclos;
chinos;
jibaros.

Gens de couleur;
sang mele—
"mixed bloods."

Chinos del pais.
Cafuso;
mameluco (mameloque);
musterfino;
metis.

Congos;
creole Negroes.

Etc., etc., etc.

African.
Slave.
Nigger.
Negro.
Colored.
Black.
African-American.

From slavery
        to freedom.
From Reconstruction
        to post-Reconstruction.
From segregation
        to Civil Rights.
From post-Civil Rights
        to post-modernism.

Living in the shadows
of this history.

XLV

America, America,
always at war,
with others,
and with herself.

Civil rights denied
brought on civil unrest.
Lawlessness,
a presidential candidate said,
inaugurating
the "war on crime,"
a war against
black people.
White lawlessness
was never challenged;
morality couldn't be
legislated.
White rage
was understandable
and accepted.
The white backlash
to black rage
was to criminalize it.

The war on poverty
turned into a
war on crime,
a war against
poor black people.
The war on crime
turned into
a war on drugs.

From pickin' cotton
        to *Cotton Comes to Harlem*
        to crack-cocaine.

Black veterans
returned from Nam
with drug habits;
they'd tried to narcotize
themselves
from the brutality of war.
They returned home
to another war,
to civil unrest,
government repression
and imprisonment.

Black veterans
beaten,
some hung.
Strange fruit,
swinging in the summer breeze.

White protesters,
students
gunned down
by National Guardsmen.
the message
was loud and clear:
we will not hesitate
to kill,
not even our own,
to enforce the Program.
Get with it!

Days of rage.

Black rage
turned on itself.
So hard to believe in
        black beauty
        when it had been debased
        and raped
        for centuries.
So hard to believe
        in black worthiness
        when it had been
        depreciated for centuries.
So hard to overcome
        the fear of whites
        when their reign of terror
        had lasted centuries
        and they proved that they
        would not share power.

White Power concedes nothing.

Confined to ghettoes.
Possibilities confined.
The dream had died
a thousand deaths,
In its wake came a
festering despair.
"What happens
to a dream deferred?"
It implodes.
Black rage
turned on itself.

"Burn, baby, burn!"

Black on black crime.
The pathology
of the colonized mind,
striking out
at what it hates
at what it has allowed itself
to become—
the wretched of the earth.

"Nigger, nigger, nigger!"
some blacks calls themselves.
This hatred internalized,
imploding.

Black bitch!
Hoochie mama.
Skeezer.
Chicken head.
'Ho.

Black women dissed
and debased
by black men.

In describing a black woman,
black men say, she's
a liar;
fickle;
hard to please;
a sneak;
a credit wrecker;
a pain in the ass;
weak;
stupid;
here to serve man;
nothing without a man;
a sexual object;
a tease;
greedy;
a heartache;
a heartbreaker;
jealous;
mouthy;
angry most of the time;
confused;
hard to handle;
a fool;
a gossipmonger;
a welfare recipient.

Black women say:
"Black men are irresponsible."
"Black men can't be trusted."
"Black men are no good."

In describing a black man,
black women say, he's
a dog;
a liar;
irresponsible;
unfaithful;
a pain in the neck;
lazy;
sloppy;
inconsiderate;
unreliable;
not to be trusted;
cheap;
a user;
manipulative;
messed up in the head;
out to take advantage of women;
hard to love;
a sex fiend;
stupid;
hard to catch;
difficult to keep;
not worth the effort;
a disappointment;
a waste of time;
a joke.

The pathology
of the colonized mind,
striking out
at what it hates,
at what it has allowed itself
to become.

"Nigger, nigger, nigger!"

XLVI

From the Harlem Renaissance
    to *A Rage in Harlem*
    to South Central L.A.

"Burn, baby, burn!"

Police brutality.
Rodney King.
The poster boy
for police brutality
against black males,
captured on video,
eighty-one seconds,
"blue knights,"
four white police officers,
fifty-six baton blows—
properly administered:
"power swings,"
"chops,"
"strokes,"
six kicks,
taser gun darts,
electronic harpoon—
racial slurs
providing background music
to this video.

Twenty-three
"'boys' in blue"
watched this action,
like extras in a movie,
didn't raise a hand
to stop this excessive
use of force—
it was a spectator sport
for them.

"Break the nigger up!"
"Do some body work!"

King's skull broken
in eleven places,
several fillings
knocked out of his teeth
because of the force
of the blows—
"power swings";
a fractured eye socket,
a broken cheekbone,
a broken leg,
facial nerve damage,
a severe concussion,
bruises all over his body,
burns from the taser gun.

"Break the nigger up!"
"Do some body work!"

The videotape evidence,
eighty-one seconds,
of police brutality.
An airtight case.
The trial in Simi Valley,
a retirement community
for cops.
Each frame,
fifty-six blows,
six kicks,
taser gun darts,
electronic harpoon,
was rationalized,
and justified.

Acquitted.
The color of justice—
lily white.

Days of rage.

From Watts
        to South Central L.A.
Both incidents linked
by police actions.

The streets are on fire.

"Burn, baby, burn!"

Black rage,
and frustration.
One acquittal too many.
"No justice, no peace.

Angry people
take to the streets.
Buildings ablaze,
shops raided.
Innocent people
set upon,
attacked.

"Burn, baby, burn!"

Days of rage.

"Can we all just get along?

"The King is dead!
Long live the King!"

XLVII

Police brutality.
A black male
sexually assaulted
by New York's Finest.
Accusations—
a plunger inserted
in his ass.
A civilian complaint
review board requested
to clean up this shit.

A black manchild,
candy bar
in silver wrapping
in hand,
emerging from a store.
He's armed,
and extremely dangerous,
even with a candy bar.

The sliver wrapping glints,
the police officer
draws his gun,
the black kid
bites the bullet.

William E. Waters ◄► 161

Another killing by cops,
justified,
the silver wrapping
on the candy bar
mistaken for a gun.

Police officers,
vigilantes with badges.
The war on crime
their justification.

Shoot first,
justify later.

Inner-city pathologies.
Media code words:
"gang-related";
"drug turf";
"crack plague";
"crack babies";
"welfare queens."

A war of words.
The "enemy" dehumanized.
Society primed
for these killings.

The big, bad black bogeyman
haunts the white imagination,
in fiction, in fact.

Othello.
Bigger Thomas.
Joe Christmas.
Emmett Till.
Willie Horton.
Central Park Attackers.
Rodney King.
Nushawn Williams.
Big, bad black bogeymen.

XLVIII

From the plantation
     to the penitentiary.
From gray uniforms
     to white robes
     to black robes
     to police and guard uniforms—
it's all about control,
control of blacks,
black males in particular.

Three strikes
and you're out—
in prison for life.

"Lock 'em up
and throw away the key!"

From Plymouth Rock
     to the Rock—
     Rikers Island:
     the largest prison
     in the Nation.

Two generations
of black males,
shackled once again.
This time with
moral justification and outrage:
"They committed crimes!"

The clanking of chains
can be heard
throughout black history
in America,
the land of the free.

The privatization of prisons—
Corrections Corporation of America.
Businessmen getting in
on the ground floor
of prison cells.
Caged cargo.
Black prisoners traded
like live stock on the
New York Stock Exchange.
From chattel to stock.
Wall Street,
brokerage houses,
financing the new
slave trade.

The new slavery
is morally justified.
They committed crimes!
Read the Thirteenth Amendment,
which abolished slavery,
replaced it with penal servitude.
Slavery shall not exist
in the United States,
and its territories,
unless duly convicted
of a crime.

From its enactment
the Thirteenth Amendment
had the re-enslavement of
blacks in mind.
The convict lease system,
chain gangs
and prison industries.
Now privatization.

Laws have always been
legislated,
enforced,
and interpreted
to curtail blacks—
from the slave codes
        to the crack-cocaine laws;
from Jim Crow
        to the Proposition of the moment.
Laws are made
specifically with blacks in mind.
Whenever these laws
are enacted,
black arrests increase.
Whenever these laws
are enacted
black rights decrease.

From the plantation
        to the penitentiary
without surcease.

XLIX

Black bodies
in prison ships,
reminiscent
of slave ships.
Barges converted
to confine black men.
The New Middle Passage.

One in three
young black males
in prison.
Fifty-one percent
of the Nation's prisoners
are black.
The United States
has the highest
reported rate of imprisonment
in the world.

On the Rock.

Young black males,
razor slashes
on their faces—
"tribal" markings—
jailhouse rage,
and hatred.

"Nigger, nigger, nigger!"

What happens to a dream deferred?
It implodes!

"Burn, baby, burn!"

Black bodies
in double-bunked
prison cells,
reminiscent
of the holding pens
off the African coast.

Screams at night
echo on
cavernous prison galleries,
remembering
the Middle Passage.

Packed prison dorms,
double-bunked beds
stretched towards low ceilings,
reminiscent
of the holds of slave ships.

Coughing at night.
Foul air.
Olfactory memories
triggered—
the stench
in the holds of slave ships.

Poor ventilation.
Horrid conditions.
Diseases.
TB.
AIDS.
Suicide.
Poverty.
Despair.

White guards
in gray uniforms,
reminiscent
of Confederate soldiers.

Psychological abuse
codified.
Physical abuse and brutality
not cruel and unusual
punishment.

Rednecks,
removed in time and place
from black reality.
Still overseeing.
Forced interaction,
a new
master/slave relationship.
Hostility on both sides.
Undocumented
and unreported violence
against black prisoners.

Courts uphold prison guards'
rights to be neo-Nazis
and Klansmen—
remember,
a Supreme Court Justice
was a Klansman.

One prison guard
proudly displays
a tattoo on his forearm
of a black man
with a noose
around his heck.
He flexes
his forearm muscle,
the black man does a dance—
the *danse macabre americain*.

Strange fruit.
Swinging in the summer breeze.

Klansmen
can wear business suits,
white robes,
black robes,
police and guard uniforms—
don't let the garb fool you!

America, America,
where blacks have
no rights
that are bound to be
respected by whites.

Angry white men
rule the world.

Skinheads.
Neo-Nazis.
Klansmen.
"Rogue" police officers.
Reactionary politicos—
fringe elements
really
in the forefront.

Police brutality.
Hate crimes.
Cross burnings.
A rash of church burnings.

"Burn, baby, burn!"

Bensonhate.
White mobs in Brooklyn,
watermelons in hands,
raised to the sky,
an offering,
to their god of hate.

"Watermelon eatin' niggers!"
"Moolies!"
"Monkeys!"
"Gorillas in the mist!"
"Coons!"
"Jigaboos!"
"Nigger, nigger, nigger!"

Immigrants.
Second and third generation.
No students of history,
no understanding
of the dark shadows
of American history.
Anti-black.
Anti-affirmative action.

"Nigger, nigger, nigger!"

Hundreds of years
on American soil.
The blood sweat and tears
of Africans fertilized
this land.

"Nigger go home!"

"This is my land, too,
I say, this is my land."

From St. Augustine
　　　　to Plymouth Rock.
From points north,
south, east and west,
blacks were there,
you could bet.

From Abraham Lincoln
　　　　to hatemongers in Bensonhurst.
The race question revisited.

The solution:
"Nigger go home!"

Forced emigration.
Voluntary emigration.
Black American
expatriates scattered
in Europe,
in Africa,
in the Caribbean—
the African Diaspora.

"Nigger go home!"

"These are my lands, too,
I say, these are my lands!"

Forcibly brought
across the Atlantic.
Hundreds of years
of forced and unpaid labor,
never compensated,
most recently apologized to
by a president
called slick Willie,
a president history'll
remember for scandals,
not his attempt
to get Americans
into a dialogue on race.

"Can we all just get along?"

In Jasper, Texas,
a black male tied
to a vehicle—
a lynching nonetheless.
Decapitated.
De-limbed.

"Nigger, nigger, nigger!"

Strange fruit,
dragged through the streets,
a black soul
ascending to "Nigger Heaven."

Copycats,
in Belleville, Illinois.
Open season on black men.

"Nigger, nigger, nigger!"

The message is loud and clear:
some white people want
niggers to go home.
Home?
Where is home?

"This is my land, too,
I say, this is my land!"

White immigrants,
second and third generation,
telling blacks to go home,
blacks who've been in
America from the
very beginning,
before Columbus,
before the Mayflower,
blacks who've fought in
every major American war.

"This is my land, too,
I say, this is my land!"

LI

Two exoduses
from the South's
reign of terror,
from Redeemers and Red Shirts:
white supremacists
with black blood
on their hands.

A reverse Migration.
From the old North
        to the New South.
Black people return and reclaim
the South as their home.
Stranger things have happened.

White people
looking for soul.
Wiggers—
white niggers.
Imitating what they think
is black culture.

Rap music—
the holy drum beat
mixed up in there
somewhere—
sampling—
barely heard over
the angry lyrics.

Broken promises,
segregation—
"hypersegregation"—
in the inner cities.
Old schools.
New state-of-the-art prisons.

Gerrymandering.
Red lining.
White flight,
to suburbia.
White flight—
Negrophobia—
of "inner-city jungles,"
of "jungle bunnies,"
of black rage.
"Fear outpacing racism,"
white social historians say.

History seemingly
repeating itself.
The New Panthers.
Retro dis and dat.

Around and around
and around we go.
Head spinning.
Hair metamorphosing.
From fried and dyed
        to jheri curls
        to dread locks
        to au natal—
        Afros.

From slavery
    to freedom
    to the new slavery.
From the plantation
    to the penitentiary
    to private prisons.

The dark shadows of history
cast across America
like a full solar eclipse,
hiding the sun,
the light of day.

The eclipse is over,
the sun shines brightly.
There's no hiding place,
not in the shadows,
not in the darkness.
The truth is in knowing,
remembering things past
and present.